D0331037

SandCastle™

First Rhymes

The Sheep Is Asleep

Kelly Doudna

Consulting Editor, Diane Craig, M.A./Reading Specialist

Publishing Company

Published by ABDO Publishing Company, 4940 Viking Drive, Edina, Minnesota 55435.

Printed in the United States.

Credits
Edited by: Pam Price
Curriculum Coordinator: Nancy Tuminelly
Cover and Interior Design and Production: Mighty Media
Photo Credits: AbleStock, Comstock, Photodisc, Stockbyte

Library of Congress Cataloging-in-Publication Data

Doudna, Kelly, 1963-
    The sheep is asleep / Kelly Doudna.
       p. cm. -- (First rhymes)
    Includes index.
    ISBN 1-59679-521-2 (hardcover)
    ISBN 1-59679-522-0 (paperback)
       1. English language--Rhyme--Juvenile literature. I. Title. II. Series.
    PE1517.D6878 2005
    808.1--dc22
                                                                    2005048113

SandCastle™ books are created by a professional team of educators, reading specialists, and content developers around five essential components that include phonemic awareness, phonics, vocabulary, text comprehension, and fluency. All books are written, reviewed, and leveled for guided reading and early intervention reading, and designed for use in shared, guided, and independent reading and writing activities to support a balanced approach to literacy instruction.

Let Us Know

After reading the book, SandCastle would like you to tell us your stories about reading. What is your favorite page? Was there something hard that you needed help with? Share the ups and downs of learning to read. We want to hear from you! To get posted on the ABDO Publishing Company Web site, send us e-mail at:

sandcastle@abdopub.com

SandCastle Level: Beginning

-eep

asleep

beep

peep

sheep

steep

She is  .

I hear a .

We hear a .

I look at the  .

The hill is .

Emma is asleep.

The clock goes beep.

PEEP!

The chick makes
a peep.

The sheep is white.

This is a steep hill.

The Sheep Is Asleep

There is a sheep.

The sheep is asleep.

18

The sheep is asleep
on a hill that is steep.

The sheep who is asleep on the hill that is steep cannot hear a bird peep.

The sheep who is asleep
on the hill that is steep
cannot hear a bird peep
or an alarm clock beep!

About SandCastle™

A professional team of educators, reading specialists, and content developers created the SandCastle™ series to support young readers as they develop reading skills and strategies and increase their general knowledge. The SandCastle™ series has four levels that correspond to early literacy development in young children. The levels are provided to help teachers and parents select the appropriate books for young readers.

Emerging Readers
(no flags)

Beginning Readers
(1 flag)

Transitional Readers
(2 flags)

Fluent Readers
(3 flags)

These levels are meant only as a guide. All levels are subject to change.

ABDO
Publishing Company

To see a complete list of SandCastle™ books and other nonfiction titles from ABDO Publishing Company, visit **www.abdopub.com** or contact us at: 4940 Viking Drive, Edina, Minnesota 55435 • 1-800-800-1312 • fax: 1-952-831-1632